# EDMUND KE

*The Life of the Co-Ed*

Copyright © 2017 by Hourly History.

# Table of Contents

# Introduction

To the average American, there was nothing out of the ordinary about Edmund Kemper before 1973. Standing at six-foot-nine, the young man was a giant, but he was gentle, soft spoken, and shy. He lived with his mother into his mid-20s and frequented local bars, cozying up to local police officers—a job he had once hoped to hold himself, but he was too tall.

This was one reality of Kemper's life—the reality he wanted those around him to see. There was another side to the man though, a much darker side. Inside his mind, Kemper lived through a series of fantasies he developed in what he called his "vicious world"—an alternative reality he created inside his mind. There, he stored his dark thoughts and fantasies about death, sex, and violent acts against women. It was where Kemper went to escape from the everyday torment he perceived his life to be. After perfecting his fantasizes over the first 24 years of his life, he was ready to start bringing them into the real world, resurrecting every gory detail of every fantasy he had.

Across 1972 and 1973, Kemper terrorized Santa Cruz and the surrounding areas of Northern California, murdering a total of eight women. He was a troubled individual who managed to keep up appearances until he lived out his ultimate fantasy: killing his own mother.

The shocking details that surround Kemper's crimes are brief windows into his soul and mind. They're incomprehensible to most humans, but for Kemper, they've been there his whole life—a life riddled with anger, pain, and loneliness.

# Chapter One

# Hatred is Born

*"I lived as an ordinary person for most of my life even though I was living a parallel increasingly sick other life."*

—Edmund Kemper

Edmund Kemper was born on December 18, 1948. His father was a World War II veteran named Edmund Emil Kemper II, who went by EE, and his mother was named Clarnell. There was always tension in the Kemper household, which also included an older and younger sister for Edmund. Clarnell's attitude dominated the home. Although EE provided a comfortable life for the family, Clarnell complained about his menial job and his passive personality persistently.

As a child, Kemper craved attention from his parents but never received much. Clarnell didn't want her son turning out to be submissive the way she saw his father, so she was strict with the young boy. Any time EE was caught showing the boy affection or kindness, he would be chastised for coddling. Kemper spent the formative years of his life feeling isolated. He had low self-esteem and felt unlovable.

In school, Kemper performed poorly. He saw teachers as extensions of his mother—he would shy away from adults, expecting the poor treatment he received from his alcoholic mother at home. His peers could tell something was off with Kemper, he was bullied mercilessly for his shyness, poor grades, and astonishing height. He had a hard time developing relationships with others throughout his life, and as a child, this meant he spent most of his time at school without friends.

In 1957, when Kemper was nine years old, his father EE left the family house for good. Kemper felt abandoned, left alone with the woman who made his life unbearable. Kemper got along with his sisters when they were younger, but as he aged and the turbulent storm brewing in his brain began to manifest in his behaviors, they quickly drifted apart. Kemper became fascinated with death. His favorite game to play with his sisters was something he called Gas Chamber, in which he would have one of his sisters throw pellets at him and lock him in a room. He would then act out suffocating to death, writhing back and forth on the floor. His sisters would play this game with him, but when Kemper became obsessed with ripping the heads off their dolls, they began to refuse, distancing themselves from the child their mother berated on a regular basis.

At this stage in his life, Kemper was unable to keep his depraved fantasies and obsessions a secret the way he was able to later as an adult. They seeped into his consciousness and had a startling effect on his actions.

At ten years old, Kemper killed his family's cat. He buried the pet alive in their backyard, and when he was sure it had died, dug it back up, removed its head, and examined its body. Several years later, Kemper repeated this ritual with the cat's replacement when he perceived the pet to be favoring his younger sister. He dismembered the second cat and stored pieces of its body in his closet as a reminder of the thrill he had felt while committing the deed.

In another incident, when Kemper was around 12 years old, he made a startling confession to his sister: like many pubescent boys his age, he had developed a crush on one of his teachers. His sister teased him for this, saying he should just kiss her to see what happens. Kemper responded that he couldn't do that. He would have to kill her first.

Clarnell Kemper was not unaware of how Edmund's behavior was developing into that of a disturbed person; she had found the rotting remnants of their second family pet in his closet after having smelt the odor of decaying flesh. Her abuse towards Kemper escalated during his early adolescence. She began locking him in the basement at night, forcing him to sleep in the cold, damp space without a bed or blankets. She said she was afraid of him coming and hurting her or her daughters in the night.

When Kemper was 15, he reached a breaking point with his mother. He couldn't take the constant verbal abuse any longer, so he left, hitchhiking to his father's home just outside of Los Angeles. He thought it would be a fresh start, but he quickly fell into old patterns. Unbeknownst to Kemper, his father had remarried since leaving Clarnell, and now had a stepson. Kemper was outraged. He felt replaced and soon began acting hostile and aggressive towards his father's new family. After one month, EE sent his son back into the arms of Clarnell.

Edmund Kemper was resistant to return to his mother's house, and he wasn't the only one. Clarnell also didn't want to accept her son back into her life. She had been happy when he had run away and told her son she had felt peace for the first time in years while he was away. She refused to take him back in and instead sent him to live with his paternal grandparents. In doing this, Clarnell was hoping to protect herself and her family from Edmund and his startling behaviors. She wanted to prevent a disaster. This decision, however, would prove to facilitate what Clarnell was trying her hardest to avoid.

# Chapter Two

# Kemper's First Murders

*"I just wanted to see how it felt to shoot Grandma."*

—Edmund Kemper

In 1963, at the age of 15, Edmund Kemper was sent to live with his paternal grandparents, Maude and Edmund Kemper I, after both of his separated parents refused to have him under their roofs. At this point in his life, Kemper was already dealing with intense feelings of loneliness and isolation from others, feelings that were perpetuated by this rejection.

Kemper's grandparents lived alone on a secluded 17-acre farm in Northern California, neatly tucked away in the mountains of North Fork. They enjoyed a peaceful life away from the cities dotted across the golden state.

Edmund Kemper got along well with his grandfather. He was a big man who worked for the highway department. He was kind, and he made an effort to spend time with Edmund. He bought Edmund a rifle so the two could go hunting together and so that the passive boy could "man up." The pair worked well together, despite Kemper's grandfather beginning to show clear signs of dementia.

While Kemper and his grandfather had a fairly stable relationship, the same could not be said of the relationship between the teenager and his grandmother. Kemper saw his grandmother as an extension of his mother. While she wasn't an alcoholic or physically abusive, Maude was high-tempered and quick to scold. As a freelance writer, Maude was used to spending days at home alone in the quiet. It was hard for her to get her work done with Edmund around, especially since Edmund required extra supervision. She was often hard on the boy, hoping to shape his behaviors into those of a more positive and productive young man.

As well as being hard on Edmund, Maude was also hard on Edmund's grandfather. Maude was used to being taken care of by her husband, who for most of their lives had been the main breadwinner in the household. As Edmund Kemper I's mental health deteriorated, the more care and help he needed from Maude, and Maude was very hard on him for this. Edmund viewed this behavior of Maude's as emasculating to his grandfather and himself. It was a repetition of the emasculation he felt and detested from Clarnell.

By August 1964, Edmund had reached a breaking point with his grandmother. He could no longer tolerate Maude's constant criticism, and his curiosity for killing had reached a point that couldn't be satiated through fantasizes or hunting.

On August 27, Kemper had been sitting in the kitchen with his grandmother when she began to chastise him, leading to an eruptive argument between the two. Kemper went outside to the farm's garage to retrieve his hunting rifle, and when he returned, he shot his grandmother once in the back of the head and twice in the back. She never saw Edmund coming.

Simply shooting his grandmother didn't satisfy the rage that consumed Edmund though. After Maude lay dead on the kitchen floor, Kemper grabbed a large knife from the kitchen drawer and began stabbing his grandmother's corpse. He couldn't kill her enough.

Several minutes later, Edmund dragged his grandmother's body into her bedroom. He knew his grandfather would be returning home from work soon, and he begun to panic. He didn't want his grandfather to see that he had killed his wife. When Edmund heard his grandfather's truck pull into the farm's driveway minutes later, he ran outside with his rifle and shot his grandfather once in the head, leaving him to bleed to death.

Through these two brutal acts, Edmund Kemper had avenged the rejection he received from his parents, all while living out his greatest fantasy and curiosity. Later, when Kemper was questioned as to why he committed these heinous acts, he gave a chilling answer: he had always wanted to know what it felt like to take a life. Now, he finally knew. What he hadn't thought through yet was what came next, what he was supposed to do after, so he did what any confused and emotionally turbulent teenager would do—he called his mother.

When she answered the phone call from Edmund, Clarnell went into shock. Seemingly out of nowhere, her son was calling her and calmly explaining that he had just murdered his two grandparents, and he didn't know what he should do next. Clarnell spoke to her son and persuaded him to call the local police and tell them what happened, and he complied. Within an hour, several officers showed up to the ranch to find the shockingly tranquil teenager waiting for them on the front porch in full view of his dead grandfather.

Edmund Kemper was immediately brought into custody. The 15-year-old never denied his actions or fought with the authorities; he was always obedient, honest, and cooperative. But it was clear that the young boy needed help to all those around him. His case was brought before a judge to decide what should be done with the youth. The judge ordered that Kemper undergo a psychiatric evaluation as a double murder was deemed incomprehensible for a boy as young as Kemper to commit willingly—he must be insane.

The court-ordered psychiatrist diagnosed Kemper with paranoid schizophrenia disorder, and he was placed in California's Atascadero State Hospital in the criminally insane unit. It was decided that Kemper would spend some time there undergoing psychiatric treatment and observation until the hospital doctors felt he was ready to be reintroduced into society.

# Chapter Three

# Institutionalized with an IQ of 145

*"I just wanted the exaltation over the party. In other words, winning over death. They were dead and I was alive. That was the victory in my case."*

—Edmund Kemper

Edmund Kemper flourished at the psychiatric hospital. It was the first time his life truly had structure, which helped him organize his actions and thoughts. At traditional schools, Kemper had struggled, but in the hospital, he excelled at learning. Doctors began to realize that Kemper was quite intelligent. Kemper had his IQ tested twice while incarcerated. The first time, Kemper scored a 136. Later, he scored a 145. This was astounding to those managing Kemper's case—both of these scores were considered to designate an individual who is intellectually gifted. Only 1% of the world's population is thought to have an IQ of 136 or above.

As Kemper began to excel more and more intellectually but also personally under state care, doctors began to question his previous diagnosis of paranoid schizophrenia. The young man wasn't suffering from hallucinations or delusions, and a true paranoid schizophrenic would have an incredibly difficult time organizing their thoughts well enough to score such a high IQ. Instead, doctors at Atascadero re-diagnosed Kemper with a passive-aggressive type personality trait disturbance.

This new diagnosis meant that doctors at the hospital believed that Kemper could be rehabilitated. Someone with a personality disorder can learn how to work with their difficulties much easier than someone with schizophrenia can. Kemper's willingness to work with doctors at the hospital also made them believe that he was working hard to become a better person, one who could succeed in the world outside of the hospital walls. Little did they know that this was Kemper's intention, and not necessarily reflective of what was going on inside Kemper's mind.

In reality, Kemper was taking this time at the hospital to learn how to conceal his urges, not work through them. He listened to doctors not to take their advice, but to learn what he needed to do and say in order to be seen as normal. Later in life, Kemper told psychiatrists that during this period of time he developed an alternative reality inside of his brain that he called his "vicious world." He learned to keep his fantasies locked away inside his brain instead of sharing them with those around him. He practiced acting rehabilitated in hopes of being able to leave the Atascadero one day.

Doctors at Atascadero had no idea what was going on inside Kemper's brain. Instead, they saw the cooperative young man they perceived Kemper to be. As Kemper appeared to become more normalized, he was given more and more responsibilities within the hospital. He began assisting doctors in administering psychiatric evaluations to other patients. He would carry psychiatric test materials unsupervised from room to room, and he later confessed that he would use these times to memorize the questions and answers that led to the psychiatrists to different conclusions about patients. He used this information to build his functioning personality and have it pass future psychiatric evaluations.

Amazingly, doctors eventually began allowing Kemper to administer parts of the evaluations or sit in during evaluations. During this time, Kemper had unfettered access to some truly deranged individuals, and he took advantage of these moments to learn and add material to his vicious world. He took mental notes, learning from sex offenders how to gain a woman's trust, how to choose victims, and other tips like that it was best to kill a woman after raping her to avoid leaving witnesses. With his intelligent brain, Kemper was good at reading between the lines of the disturbed individuals. He would listen to their accounts of their crimes and turn the information into a how-to guide of sorts, all while convincing doctors he was overcoming his dark urges and desires. He had perfected the art of the secret personality.

# Chapter Four

# Back with His Mother

*"I couldn't please her. It was like being in jail. I became a walking time bomb and I finally blew . . . It was like that the second time, with my mother."*

—Edmund Kemper

In 1969, after five years of being incarcerated, Edmund Kemper was deemed ready to be reintroduced into society by the Atascadero State Hospital's team of psychiatrists. They had one strong recommendation upon his release: Kemper should not be released back into the custody of his mother. As well as Kemper could conceal the sinister thoughts inside his mind, he couldn't conceal the hatred he still had for Clarnell.

On December 18, 1969, his 21st birthday, Edmund Kemper was officially released from the Atascadero State Hospital. He was required to attend parole meetings and further psychiatric monitoring, but doctors were confident he would be able to lead a fulfilling life.

The California State Authority was in charge of deciding where the troubled young man would go after his release. Although he was 21, he was not ready to live alone. He didn't have any money or job prospects, so he wasn't able to support himself. Fraught with few options, the state authority decided to place Kemper back into the care of his mother, despite the recommendation made by Kemper's team at Atascadero.

While Edmund was incarcerated, Clarnell had moved to a small suburb just outside of Santa Cruz, California. She worked for the University of California Santa Cruz as an administrator and had a comfortable life. At first, the mother and son got along, but it was only a month or so before their relationship soured again. Kemper felt like his mom was too dominating, she treated him like he was broken, pathetic. He felt like an idiot, a throwback to his tumultuous childhood, after having built a sense of self-respect for the first time in his life.

Life outside of Atascadero was difficult for Kemper. He craved structure in his life but didn't know how to establish this for himself, especially as his mental health began deteriorating again in the wake of moving back in with Clarnell.

To make matters worse, Santa Cruz itself had transformed into a rebellious world of sex, drugs, and protests while Edmund had been in the state hospital. It was chaotic and filled with rampant young people who were ready to fight for whatever they believed. Edmund hated this chaos, which mirrored the maelstrom inside his mind. In turn, he began hating the young students he perceived as being the cause of all the commotion.

Another condition of Kemper's release from Atascadero was that he needed to participate in secondary education, so Kemper enrolled in a local community college. Kemper desperately wanted to fight the rebellion around him by working in law enforcement, so he began taking criminology courses. The fact that Kemper had committed a double homicide as a youth didn't disqualify him from working as a police officer; his criminal records had been sealed since he was a minor at the time of the crime. He worked hard and achieved good grades, only to find out later when he applied to become a state trooper that standing at six-foot-nine, he was too tall. Kemper's height was outside of the parameters being accepted for law enforcement at the time.

This discovery was a huge blow to Kemper, who was still self-conscious about his size after being teased about it his whole life. But he was determined to get out of his mother's house, and he knew he needed a job to do this. Kemper secured a position with the California highway department, taking after his grandfather who he had killed years before.

Kemper enjoyed his time working with the highway department. His size became an advantage to him for the first time, as it helped him to excel at the physical labor. It was menial but structured, and it kept him busy during the day. After several months of hard work, Kemper had saved up enough money to become financially independent for the first time in his life. With the blessing of his parole officer, Kemper left his mother's home and moved into an apartment in Alameda, a 90-minute drive from Santa Cruz.

In Alameda, Kemper continued to work for the highway department, but independence in his personal life left him with too much free time for his own good. By all accounts, he was living a normal life, but he still felt like his mother was domineering over him. She regularly phoned him and paid him surprise visits to check in on him. It fed the notion that he could never truly get away from Clarnell, no matter how much distance he put between them.

With this continued frustration, Kemper's inner demons became agitated, they were getting ready to resurface. Kemper couldn't shake the feeling of inferiority his mother gave him, and when he was provoked by his hatred for Clarnell, the only thing that seemed to suppress the rage was fantasizing about acts of violence and anger again. And fantasizing was quickly becoming insufficient. He knew it wouldn't be long before he would need to start acting on these desires to quell his intense fury.

Edmund Kemper's turbulent relationship with his mother did more than just agitate his inner rage though; it also set up a pattern for his future relationships with women throughout his life. Kemper was afraid of women. He felt awkward and irritated around them although he craved companionship. The more awkward he got around women, the more he began to resent them. A healthy relationship with a woman was the prize in life he knew he would never achieve.

Kemper did manage to maintain one long-term relationship in his life. Right after moving to Alameda, Kemper, who was in his early 20s, began dating a 16-year-old girl who attended the local high school. The pair dated for a while and eventually became engaged. His mother highly disapproved of the match, and Clarnell harassed her son until the couple parted. She berated him for dating someone so young. When Kemper asked his mother to introduce him to ladies his own age from the university she worked at, she refused, telling Edmund that he was too much like his father—he didn't deserve to get to know them.

Although he knew he would never become a police officer himself, Kemper found a way to stay connected with the world of criminology. He began visiting several bars around Alameda after work. His favorite became the Jury Room, a bar known to be frequented by police officers. Kemper would stop by the Jury Room almost every day after work, making an effort to cozy up to the cops.

The police officers soon became familiar with the large man who made an impression. Kemper developed a persona he later characterized as a happy nuisance to buddy up with the officers and hear about the cases they were working on and other aspects of their jobs. The police officers all liked Kemper. They found him to be polite and soft-spoken—a gentle giant of sorts. When they got together to unwind and talk about their days, they didn't mind having him around listening. They didn't think it could cause any harm. What they didn't know was that Kemper was smart enough to be taking mental notes, he paid attention to the logic behind their actions so he could predict how the officers would react to any situation.

By spring of 1972, Edmund's desire to begin acting out his violent fantasies was growing out of control. He had lost his job with the highway service and was running out of money. Fearing that he'd soon have to move back in with Clarnell, he began planning violent acts in detail to soothe his inner anger. Even this wasn't enough anymore though—he needed to start acting on his urges.

The urge that Kemper wanted to act out most of all, whether he realized it at the time or not, was to kill his mother. Clarnell was the antagonizing cause of his hatred and fear of women. Kemper never felt accepted by his mother, and therefore could not see himself ever being accepted by another woman.

But Kemper wasn't emotionally ready to kill his mother. He still relied on her to survive, she helped him out financially when he got in trouble, and since he'd lost his job, he knew it was just a matter of time before he'd need to live with her again. And, even to someone as disturbed as Kemper, seriously thinking about killing his mother was too much for his psyche to bear. Kemper was fantasizing about killing Clarnell but never thought he could actually do it. So instead, he fantasized about killing women in general.

Over the next year, Kemper embarked on a murderous journey that ended when, as he has stated, he was honest with himself for the first time and killed his mother.

# Chapter Five

# Realizing His Fantasies

*"At first I picked up girls just to talk to them, just to try to get acquainted with people my own age and try to strike up a friendship."*

—Edmund Kemper

Before Edmund Kemper realized he wanted to kill his mother, he knew he wanted to hurt women. He also knew that as an awkward 23-year-old, he didn't have a good chance of approaching potential victims outright, and ambushing women didn't play into his fantasies. He wanted them to trust him before he killed them.

Kemper's preferred victims were young university students or co-eds. California seemed to be teeming with young students, who often hitchhiked to get around. Kemper saw an endless supply of hitchhiking women when he worked for the highway department. They would be easy targets for him. He just needed to figure out how to make them feel safe enough to get into a car with him.

Fixating on the fantasy of picking up a hitchhiking student for his murderous plans, Kemper began driving his Ford Galaxie up and down highways, often for hours at end, surveying his potential victims. He was slowly building up the nerve to pull over and offer one a ride.

Eventually, Kemper got up the courage. This event was the opening of a floodgate. Over the next few months, Kemper picked up over 150 female hitchhikers for the sole purpose of practicing his social skills on them. He developed techniques on how to pick up the women, how to make them feel more comfortable around him, and how to make them trust him. He would watch the women carefully, noting their reactions to different things he said or did, and he paid attention to where their strengths and weaknesses lied. He found ways to increase the women's vulnerability while decreasing opportunities for them to get the upper hand over himself.

As he got more confident offering rides to women, he began storing tools in his trunk such as plastic bags, knives, blankets, and handcuffs. He rigged his passenger door so that it couldn't be opened from the inside anymore. Once inside, passengers had no way out unless Kemper allowed them to exit the vehicle. He even built up the nerve to bring a gun into the front of the vehicle, hiding it beneath his leg or under his seat, proving to himself that a future victim would never know it was there until it was too late.

On May 7, 1972, Kemper felt prepared enough to put his planning into place. Fueled by rage after a fight over the phone with his mother, Kemper set out into the evening to pick up some hitchhikers. This time was different though—he was no longer just practicing.

Kemper came across two students who were hitchhiking from Fresno State College to Stanford, where they planned to visit with some friends. The two girls were

Mary Ann Pesce and Anita Luchessa, both 18 years old. Kemper picked the girls up from the side of the highway and set off, promising to deliver them at their intended location. He talked to the girls and made them feel safe, so they didn't notice when he began veering off the course to Stanford.

Kemper brought the two young women to a secluded wooded area just outside of Alameda. He had discovered the location while working for the highway department. When the girls finally realized that something was wrong, they began to panic. To calm them down, Kemper promised Pesce that he would drop both girls back off on the highway safely if she followed his demands. Pesce complied.

Kemper ordered Pesce out of the car, leaving Luchessa locked alone inside the car. He brought Pesce to the back of the car and opened up the trunk. He grabbed a knife and a plastic bag from his kit of supplies and forced Pesce inside. Pesce knew she was in danger and began to fight back, breaking one of Kemper's taillights. She no longer believed that he had any intention of keeping either woman alive.

Kemper tried to suffocate Pesce by placing a plastic bag over her head, but she managed to rip a hole through it during her struggle with her large attacker. Kemper, feeling he was quickly losing control over the situation, then stabbed the young woman several times until she could no longer fight back. He then returned to the vehicle and slit Anita Mary Luchessa's throat, knowing that he would need to kill the young woman quickly to avoid another fight.

After killing these two women, Kemper felt unsatisfied. The night had not gone the way he had hoped for. He had wanted to spend more time with the two girls before killing them, and having Pesce fight back made him feel emasculated. He had experienced another awkward moment during the night as well. When he later told officers about this crime, he mentioned that at one point his hand brushed against Pesce's breast. He had felt extremely embarrassed and apologized for it profusely, despite the fact that he knew he would be killing her minutes later.

After murdering Luchessa, Kemper put her body in the trunk of his car along with Pesce's body. He took a few minutes to regain his composure, as he was shaky and filled with adrenaline. He managed to calm himself down quite effectively.

During his drive home, he was stopped by a police officer for having a broken tail light. Kemper and the officer spoke briefly, and Kemper convinced the policeman to let him off with a warning. Unbeknownst to the officer, behind the broken tail light in Kemper's trunk were the bodies of two young women he had just murdered.

Kemper brought both bodies back to his apartment in Alameda. After spending most of his life obsessed with death, he now had the opportunity to explore it first-hand for himself. Both bodies were brought into Kemper's house, and there, Kemper had sex with them. He also took a series of pornographic photos of the two dead women, wanting to preserve the memories.

Kemper took his time with the bodies. It was two days before he finally dismembered the two corpses and wrapped each part up in plastic bags. He brought the body parts to Loma Prieta Mountain, where he scattered them around, a technique he had learned to use by watching police shows on TV. By scattering the body parts, he knew there was a smaller chance that all of the parts could be found or that either body could be identified.

Kemper disposed of the two women's heads last, engaging in oral sex with them first.

Kemper fixated on women's heads. To him, it was where the very essence of a person was held. The heads possessed the ability to think, see, and speak. It was where all judgments were held, made, and expressed. By removing women's heads, Kemper was controlling them completely. He was taking away their ability to reject him. They were no longer a human; they were a living doll for him to play with.

Mary Ann Pesce and Anita Luchessa were reported missing by their parents after they never returned from visiting friends in Stanford. Police initially disregarded the two girls' disappearance. Students running away was very common at the time. Hitchhikers could catch a ride to anywhere, and many went out with the sole purpose of finding a new life. The police could not afford to spend time looking for young people who didn't want to be found.

This enraged the Pesce and Luchessa families, who didn't believe that Mary Ann and Anita had run away. Anita Luchessa's father hired a private investigator to look into Anita's disappearance, but the investigator had little to go off. All he knew was the Luchessa had set out that night looking to hitch a ride and was never seen again. Without knowing who had picked her up, there was little else anyone could find out, and there was no physical evidence to suggest that either girl was definitively alive or dead.

Kemper's plan of scattering the body parts continued to work for two-and-a-half months until a hiker stumbled upon Mary Ann Pesce's decomposed head in the mountains near Santa Cruz. Her identity was confirmed by dental records. No other body parts from either woman were found. Even though they now knew that both women had been murdered, the police still weren't able to investigate the two crimes. No other evidence was ever recovered.

# Chapter Six

# The Struggle for Control

*"I suppose as I was standing there looking, I was doing one of those triumphant things, too, admiring my work and admiring her beauty, and I might say admiring my catch like a fisherman."*

—Edmund Kemper

Mary Ann Pesce and Anita Luchessa's murders set a disturbing pattern for the future crimes of Edmund Kemper. He replayed the encounter over and over in his head, fantasizing about them, but also learning from the experience. It wasn't long before he was planning his next murder, fine-tuning his plan based on what had gone right and what had gone wrong.

Four long months later, Edmund Kemper struck again. This time, he wasn't fueled by rage but by opportunity. While driving home one night, he saw a young, petite girl hitchhiking alone in the dark at a bus stop. The girl, 15-year-old Aiko Koo, explained to Kemper that she had missed the bus to a dance class and had no way of letting anyone know. To Kemper, it was too ideal to pass up.

Kemper told Koo that he could drive her to her dance class no problem. He was heading that way anyways and understood that she was in a real bind. Koo got into his car.

One thing Kemper regretted from his last murder was that he had felt that he had little control over his victims before they had died. It had dampened his fantasies for him, and he wanted to make sure that never happened again. He wanted his new victim to trust him right until the moment he killed her.

Kemper drove Aiko Koo to a remote location and explained to her that she was being kidnapped. As he had expected, Koo became hysterical. This was when the real challenge began for Kemper. He wanted to talk her down, prove that he was a good person, and just when Koo was at her most vulnerable he would strike.

Unfortunately for Koo, Kemper was very good with words—he had been practicing what to say for months now. Kemper explained to the young girl that initially when he had picked her up, he had wanted to kill himself and take her with him. He was severely depressed and didn't want to die alone. But he had changed since then. Since speaking to her during their car ride together, he had decided that she deserved to live. Now, he just wanted to talk to her for a while.

The two began to talk, and Koo believed she was negotiating for her life. Although no one will never know exactly what was said in that car, it is known that Kemper was incredibly convincing and that Koo felt safe with Kemper. At one point during the interaction, Kemper got out of the car to retrieve something from his trunk. He was getting ready to kill Koo, and he was getting so excited and anxious that he managed to lock himself out of the car with Koo safely inside. This could've been disastrous for Kemper; however, he was able to talk Koo into letting him back in.

The choice to let Kemper back into the vehicle was the last choice Koo ever got to make. After getting back inside the car, Kemper choked Koo until she fell unconscious. He raped her and then strangled her to death with her scarf.

After putting Koo's body into his trunk, Kemper drove to a nearby bar and had a couple of drinks. He told investigators later that he remembered going into the parking lot after he was finished, opening up the trunk of his car and admiring his catch like a fisherman. This kill made him feel proud. Despite a few bumps in the road, things had gone according to his plan. He had been dominating; he had taken control. He felt like a man.

This crime was also a landmark for Edmund Kemper; he was now officially a serial killer. He had committed three murders now over the period of several months with a cooling off period in between where Kemper returned to a life of normalcy. Kemper, like many other infamous serial killers, had also established a routine or ritual following his murders with this crime.

After killing Koo, he brought her body back to his apartment where he removed her head. He had sex with her body and spent several days with it before finally dismembering it and scattering the limbs across several deserted locations.

# Chapter Seven

# Kemper Escalates

*"When I see a pretty girl walking down the street, I think two things. One part wants to be real nice and sweet, and the other part wonders what her head would look like on a stick."*

—Edmund Kemper

While committing these atrocious acts, Kemper was able to keep up appearances to the outside world. He continued to spend a lot of time with police officers and continued to attend psychiatric appointments that were a condition of his parole after being released from the Atascadero State Hospital three years earlier.

The day after he murdered Aiko Koo, Edmund Kemper attended one of his routine appointments with his psychiatrist. This appointment became incredibly significant for the young man. During this session, it was revealed to Kemper that the court no longer believed he needed to remain on parole. He had satisfied them enough that he would no longer need to attend meetings with his psychiatrist and his criminal record from his youth would be officially expunged.

The psychiatrists overseeing Kemper during his parole believed that Kemper had successfully found a way to deal with whatever had been plaguing him enough to kill his grandparents as a youth. They believed he was now living a typical life. This couldn't have been further from the truth. Kemper had mastered hiding his dark desires and terrifying crimes from the public and those who were responsible for monitoring him. While this meeting took place, Aiko Koo's dismembered head was sitting in his car trunk outside.

Aiko Koo was reported missing by her mother the same night Kemper picked her up from the bus stop, but her disappearance was never investigated. Koo's mother tried to look for answers, plastering the area where Koo disappeared with flyers, but she never received any information or calls back. Koo's remains were never found.

Shortly after murdering Aiko Koo, Edmund Kemper ran out of money. Without anywhere else to turn, he was forced to move back in with his mother, Clarnell, who welcomed him reluctantly. The two had spent their whole lives at odds with one another, and they fought constantly.

It was incredibly difficult for Kemper to be around his mother. Their fighting wore down on his confidence which in turn deteriorated his mental health. When his mental health wore down, Kemper had a harder time concealing his dark fantasies. He began to act stranger, making it more difficult for him to acquire or keep a job, which in turn made him feel stuck. Without money, Kemper couldn't leave his mother's house. But without leaving his mother's house, he couldn't work up the strength to keep up his normalcy. It was a vicious cycle.

Moving back in with Clarnell was the beginning of the end for Kemper. His internal and external realities were beginning to intertwine, and although he was still fighting to live normally, Kemper knew it was only a matter of time before he would need to take his next victim.

One of the things that Kemper's mother was especially hard on him for was his inability to maintain a relationship with a girlfriend. It was a sensitive subject for Kemper, and he detested when his mom would bring it up, as he blamed her directly for making him so unable to connect with women. Kemper had only maintained one relationship in his life, and it was with a teenager. His mom wanted him to get a new girlfriend but refused to introduce him to anyone.

Kemper later told police officers that he wanted a relationship with a woman badly. He craved having someone to love and to love him in return, but it never seemed to coincide with either of his realities. It caused him a lot of chaos inside his mind. He would see a pretty girl walking down the street or a couple out on a date, and he would want that very badly. His brain was filled with dichotomies, and the dichotomies just served to anger him more. He couldn't get away from the yelling; it was coming from inside his mind.

On January 7, 1973, Edmund Kemper set out to quiet some of the rage swelling in his brain by finding his next victim. Kemper enjoyed preying on college students, probably because the college connection made them better representatives for his mother, who also worked at a prominent California university.

On this day, Kemper was patrolling through the Cabrillo College campus when he found Cindy Schall, an 18-year-old student hitchhiking. Schall initially was reluctant to get into a car with a man as large as Kemper. There had been a lot of young woman going missing recently, as Kemper wasn't the only serial killer operating in the Santa Cruz region at the time, and she didn't think she'd stand a chance against Kemper if something went wrong.

After a few minutes of chatting though, Kemper secured Schall's trust, and she got into his car. Following the same pattern as his previous murders, Kemper drove Schall out to a remote location. He then revealed a gun he had hidden underneath the driver's seat. According to Kemper, he then got out of the car and left the gun inside with Cindy, giving her a chance to escape. Instead, she went to the trunk and asked to get inside.

This account of what happened with Cindy Schall is undoubtedly false, which is uncharacteristic of Edmund Kemper, who has been shockingly honest and forthcoming with investigators and psychiatrists about his crimes in recent years. Psychiatrists have claimed that there are two likely scenarios for why Kemper's account of this murder, in particular, is so bizarre. Either something happened during the murder of Schall that Kemper was incredibly embarrassed or ashamed of, or Kemper was so mentally frail that during the murder he perceived the events taking place to be one of his fantasizes, thus skewing his belief of what actually took place. He was shrinking deeper and deeper into his fantasy world.

What investigators do know for sure, is that Kemper shot Cindy in the head, killing her instantly. He then drove her to his mother's house, where Clarnell was sleeping inside. Not wanting to be detected by his mother, Kemper hid Schall's body in his closet overnight, waiting for his mother to leave for work the next day before attempting to do anything further.

When Kemper was eventually alone in the house, he had sex with Schall's body several times, removed the bullet from her head to avoid detection, and then beheaded and dismembered her body in his mother's bathtub. Kemper disposed of Schall's body parts by driving up the coast and dumping the parts along the way into the Pacific Ocean, except for Schall's head, which he kept for several days hidden in his closet. He performed oral sex with Schall's dismembered head during this time and then eventually buried it face-up in his mother's yard, stating that Clarnell would like it that way—she always liked having people looking up at her.

Cindy Schall's dismembered body was discovered along the coastline within 24 hours. All parts were recovered except for Schall's head and right hand. It was the least careful Kemper had ever been while disposing of a victim. Because it hadn't taken long for the body to be recovered, pathologists were able to complete an examination of the body. It was determined that she had been shot and then stabbed to death several times with a large kitchen knife, before being cut into pieces using a power saw. It painted a horrific picture for police.

# Chapter Eight

# The Two Active Serial Killers in California

*"We serial killers are your sons, we are your husbands, we are everywhere. And there will be more of your children dead tomorrow."*

—Ted Bundy

By the time he had murdered Cindy Schall, Kemper had been responsible for the deaths of four co-ed women all from the same area of Northern California in less than a year. Police knew that they had a problem on their hands, but several factors made it difficult for them to realize exactly what they were dealing with.

First of all, many co-eds were going missing that weren't being murdered. This was a consequence of the rebellious culture that was present in Santa Cruz and the surrounding areas at the time. Young people often just got up and left, looking for adventure or whatever came their way.

Second of all, and most incredibly, Edmund Kemper wasn't the only serial killer operating in Northern California at the time. Herbert Mullin, who was born in Salinas, California, just outside of the Greater Bay Area, was another notorious serial killer who killed 13 people between October 1972 and February 1973.

Mullin was a deranged individual. He was a true paranoid schizophrenic who claimed that voices in his head told him that the most devastating earthquake ever to hit California was imminent, but he could prevent it by sacrificing humans. He was fearless with his actions, he attacked random individuals, often in broad daylight. His victims had no pattern. They included a man mowing his lawn, a mother and her two daughters camping in the mountains, and many others who were simply walking down the street. In one particular event, Mullin killed a female college student and dismembered her body, possibly following in Kemper's footsteps, almost as if he was trying out something new that was working for someone else, like a colleague.

Mullin and Kemper were later imprisoned together. According to those around them, Mullin acted as if he had a crush on Kemper in prison. He was always trying to be his friend or talk to him about what they had done. Kemper never returned the friendship though and found the man to be annoying.

Having two serial killers on their hands overwhelmed Santa Cruz police, and while Mullin was also killing, they weren't sure if they were dealing with more than one individual. When Mullin was arrested in 1973 after being seen shooting someone on the street in broad daylight, they thought that the killings would stop. But the same month of Mullin's arrest, the dismembered remains of two more college co-eds were found spread across Eden Canyon and along Highway 1 in Northern California.

The remains found were from Kemper's next two victims: 23-year-old Rosalind Thorpe and 20-year-old Allison Liu. Kemper picked up the two hitchhikers on February 5, 1973, from the University of California Santa Cruz's campus, where his mother worked. Kemper had set off looking for victims after another significant blow-out with his mother. It was one of the worst fights the pair had had yet, spurring Kemper to kill again much sooner than usual and to find a victim from a location that felt more personal than usual.

# Chapter Nine

# The Co-Ed Killer

*"I was the hunter and they were the victims."*

—Edmund Kemper

After Cindy Schall's brutally murdered remains were uncovered, it was clear to many people that hitchhiking students were being targeted for violent crimes. The University of California, along with many other institutions in the area, urged students not to get into the vehicle of anyone they didn't know, or if they were going to hitchhike, only get into vehicles that had a "U of C" sticker on the bumper. These stickers designated that the individual driving was connected with the university and therefore not the killer.

This logic, however, was flawed. The day that Rosalind Thorpe and Allison Liu got into the car with Kemper, he had a university sticker on his bumper, which had been given to him by his mother as he often drove her to and from work. The two girls were following precautions, thinking they would be safe. It wasn't long before they learned that that wasn't the case.

Edmund Kemper shot and killed Thorpe and Liu in the backseat of his car before he had even left the university campus. He wrapped their bodies up in blankets and moved them into his trunk. He then took the bodies directly to his mother's house, where outside the building he beheaded the two corpses. He was getting confident in his actions; he felt in control of the world. Kemper later told investigators that while he was beheading the two women, he could see his neighbors sitting in their living room watching television. If they had turned around at the right time, they would've seen what he was doing, but he didn't care anymore.

After beheading the women in his trunk, Kemper carried their bodies inside the house while his mother slept. He had sex with them, removed the bullets, and hid them in his closet. The next day when he was alone, he dismembered the bodies and scattered the remains along Highway 1 and Eden Canyon. The remains at Eden Canyon were discovered only a week later, and the remains along the highway were found the next month.

Edmund Kemper was now at his most confident. He felt invincible. His crimes were now distinct from those of Herbert Mullin, and they were being featured heavily in the media. All of California and the rest of America were being bombarded with headlines featuring the crimes of the killer who was now being dubbed the Co-Ed Killer.

Kemper enjoyed the attention; it gave him confidence in other areas of his life. It was the first time he perceived himself as successful at something, and people were recognizing his success for the first time. Meanwhile, Kemper was able to continue his day-to-day life undetected. Although at times he grew paranoid that the police were on to him, there was no logical evidence for this. He had never been approached about the murders, and even when others around him talked about the news, he intentionally wouldn't engage. He always listened, taking mental notes on what people thought was happening, and how he could further deflect attention away from himself. Kemper enjoyed the fearful hold he had over Northern California.

## Chapter Ten

# Kemper's Grand Finale: The Death of His Mother

*"It was an urge. . . . A strong urge, and the longer I let it go the stronger it got, to where I was taking risks to go out and kill people—risks that normally, according to my little rules of operation, I wouldn't take because they could lead to arrest."*

—Edmund Kemper

On April 2, 1983, Kemper decided to upgrade his weapons arsenal. He never really cared about the method he used to kill women, it was more about what he did after they were dead to him. But for the first time in his killing career, Kemper felt ready to move up. He wanted to buy a .44 Magnum revolver. He thought it would make him feel more powerful than his current .22 caliber handgun.

Kemper was able to walk into a firearms store and purchase the revolver. Because his youth records had been expunged, the store owner had no way of knowing that he was a convicted criminal. However, when a request for a proper background check was released to police, the police were able to see that he had a youth record for a double homicide. They decided that they needed to do a more thorough check on Kemper, which normally took several weeks. In the meantime, they wanted to remove the weapon from Kemper's possession temporarily until the check came back clear.

The day after Kemper purchased the revolver, police officers knocked on his door to confiscate it. Kemper was compliant and surrendered the weapon without incident. The officers joked with the man and assured him that this procedure was purely protocol, and it was. The officers visiting his house had no idea that the large man on the other side of the door was the serial killer they were desperately trying to find.

This incident shook Kemper's new-found confidence. Although the officers had been assuring that everything was fine, Kemper couldn't shake the paranoia that told him that the cops were surely on to him now. Over the next few weeks, Kemper became more and more paranoid and had begun to lose his sense of rational thought. He began perceiving everything around him as a sign of his imminent capture. He was spiraling fast.

It was during this paranoid spiral that Edmund Kemper's murderous rage came to an all-time high, and he committed the deed that he'd been practicing for his whole life: killing his mother, Clarnell.

On April 20, 1973, Edmund Kemper was asleep at home on the couch while the 52-year-old Clarnell was away at a party. Kemper woke up when Clarnell arrived home, and she began to berate him, saying that she supposed he wanted to sit up all night and talk. Kemper said no, that wasn't his intention, and Clarnell went up to bed. But Kemper felt emasculated. He felt like a small child again and realized for the first time that he wanted to kill Clarnell. To him, it was what everything in his life had been leading up to. When he decided to kill his mother, he felt like he was honest with himself for the first time in his life.

Kemper waited downstairs until he was sure Clarnell had fallen asleep. When he was sure she was passed out, he grabbed a claw hammer, went into Clarnell's room, and beat her to death, releasing years of pent up anger and resentment. When he was finished, he realized he had finally succeeded in getting his mother out of his life for good. But he wasn't done yet.

Kemper decapitated Clarnell's corpse and engaged in oral sex with her dismembered head before placing it on a shelf and using it as a dartboard. He smashed her face in and removed her larynx and tongue, shoving both down through the garbage disposal afterward. He had sex with his mother's corpse, hid it in a closet, and went out for a drink.

While he was drinking at the bar, Kemper had a thought. Clarnell's murder was going to point straight to him as the culprit, so he devised a plan to make the crime look like it had been committed by an intruder. He went back to the house and called Clarnell's best friend Sally Hallett, and invited her over on his mother's behalf. When Hallett arrived at the house, Kemper approached her like he was giving her a welcoming hug, but instead strangled her to death with the scarf she was wearing. He then decapitated the corpse and spent the night with her body.

The next day, Edmund Kemper fled town. He was sure he was going to be discovered as the Co-Ed Killer after his last two murders, so he drove east for three days in Hallett's car, stopping in Pueblo, California. Along the way, Kemper avidly listened to the radio, hoping to hear news about his mother's death and who the police thought was responsible, but he heard nothing. The crime hadn't yet been discovered, and the police had no idea that Kemper was the killer.

After several days of running, Kemper gave up. He decided that he didn't want to be on the run anymore. Psychologically, he felt like he had completed his life's mission, and he had started to become annoyed that he hadn't been given any recognition yet. As well, he knew he had no means of survival without his mother. Kemper needed money and structure, and he knew he couldn't do it by himself. He had realized he was running, but he had nowhere to go. He was the same scared kid who'd just killed his grandparents but didn't know what to do, except this time he couldn't call his mom. Instead, he called the Santa Cruz police.

# Conclusion

# Arrest, Imprisonment, and Parole

*"His feeling is that he—and this is his belief—no one's ever going to let him out and he's just happy, he's just as happy going about his life in prison."*

—Scott Currey, Kemper's attorney

The police officer who answered Edmund Kemper's call knew the man well, and also knew that he liked to drink heavily. Because of this, when Kemper called and confessed to the murder of his mother as well as seven other women, the officer thought Kemper was joking and hung up the phone. Outraged, Kemper called back and spoke to Officer Jim Connor, another drinking buddy of his. This time though, Kemper began revealing details about the co-ed murders that only the killer could have known. He insisted the officers visit his mother's house to see exactly what he had done.

Officer Connor stayed on the phone with Kemper while another team went out to Clarnell's house to see if Kemper was telling the truth. When they entered, they found a gruesome scene. Kemper stayed at the phone booth until Pueblo police picked him up and brought him to Colorado, where he was picked up by Santa Cruz police the next day. During the drive back to Santa Cruz, Kemper began confessing to all of his murders in such gory detail that the officers asked him to stop.

On May 7, 1973, Edmund Kemper was formally charged with eight counts of first-degree murder. There was no question that Kemper had been the murderer they were after, but Kemper and his attorney Jim Jackson entered a plea of not guilty by reason of insanity.

Kemper's trial began on October 23, 1973. During the trial, Kemper's confessional tapes were played in full to the horror of those attending the court. The court-appointed psychiatrist revealed his strong belief that Kemper was legally sane now and at the times of his crimes. Further, he stated that he believed Kemper had begun to enjoy the infamy associated with being labeled a serial killer. It took the jury only five hours to agree that Kemper was both sane and guilty on all eight counts.

Edmund Kemper was given a sentence of seven years to life for each count of murder to be served concurrently at the California Medical Facility. He asked to be given the death penalty, but this was ignored.

Similar to his time at Atascadero, Kemper has been thriving in prison. He enjoys the structure that incarceration brings him, and he is considered to be a model inmate. He has never had a disciplinary hearing. He has been given several important responsibilities while incarcerated, including scheduling appointments for the prison's psychiatrists. Kemper also spends his time working with clay and ceramics and has received praise for his craftsmanship of ceramic mugs. He also is one of the most prolific narrators of books on tape for the blind.

Because of his model behavior in prison, Kemper became eligible for parole in 1979. When he met with the parole board assigned to him, he told them that he did not feel ready to be released. He is happy to go about his life in prison and doesn't trust himself in the outside world. It's a place he doesn't understand, and he doesn't think he ever will. He has said the same thing to different parole boards fourteen times between then and 2017.

During his time behind bars, Kemper has participated in several prison interviews, some taped and some private, to contribute to understanding the mind of serial killers. He has said that he wants to save others like himself from killing. If someone had understood him for who he truly was when he was younger, he might not have fallen down the same path. He destroyed his own life as well as the lives of ten other people.

12437795R00028

Printed in Great Britain
by Amazon